HOW
TO NOT
SUCK
at PRESENTATIONS

Transform Your
Presentation Skills from
BORING to **BADASS**

HOW TO NOT

SUCK

at PRESENTATIONS

Transform Your
Presentation Skills from
BORING to **BADASS**

FERN CHAN

FERN CHAN

FERN CHAN

ISBN - e-book: 978-1-7379388-0-4
ISBN - paperback: 978-1-7379388-1-1
ISBN - audiobook: 978-1-7379388-2-8

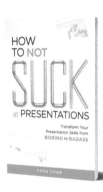

This book is dedicated to my husband William,
whose unwavering love and support made this possible.

TABLE OF **CONTENTS**

Introduction

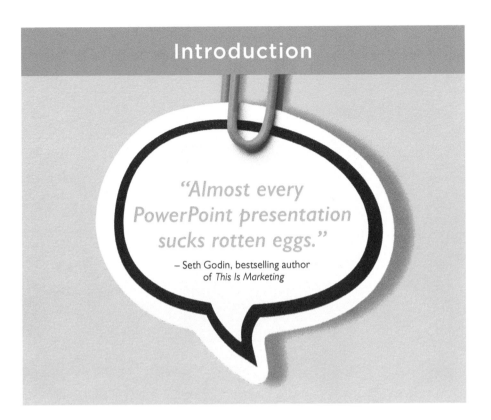

"Almost every
PowerPoint presentation
sucks rotten eggs."

– Seth Godin, bestselling author
of *This Is Marketing*

T.M.I. Too much information. This is the crisis we face in today's digital age. We are so used to information overload that we can't help but return the favor tenfold when we present information of any kind. And what do most people use to deliver their presentations? Our friend PowerPoint. Since its creation in 1987, PowerPoint has become synonymous with presenting, and standard practice is to prepare a slide deck for any kind of presentation. There's definitely no shortage of opportunities to present information. Whether you are a student presenting a project, a business owner pitching a product, or a subject-matter expert speaking at a conference among peers, there will always be a captive audience. Yet 30 years and millions of PowerPoint presentations later, it is a wonder so many people still suck at presenting.

If you use PowerPoint in any way, shape, or form, how are you using it to communicate information to others? Do you think you are getting your point across? Are you giving too much information? Would you like to see more engagement from the audience? Would you like to set yourself apart from those who suck? If any of these questions apply to you, then read on. I have a special mission for you. The objective is clear enough. You have a message to convey. You want it to stick in your audience's mind. Your mission (should you choose to accept it) is to:

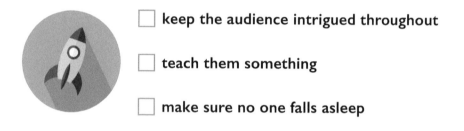

☐ **keep the audience intrigued throughout**

☐ **teach them something**

☐ **make sure no one falls asleep**

Sounds easy enough. But before you accept this mission, let's do a little reconnaissance as an audience member.

SCENARIO:

You are at a conference, barely awake in the current session. There are copious lines of text and bullet points as the presenter reads off the slides verbatim. You're thinking to yourself with a hint of frustration, *If all he had to do was stand there and read the slide, then why on earth am I paying for this? I could read off the slide!* But you hang in there out of courtesy with the meager hope that the presentation will improve. It doesn't. The onslaught continues with cheesy clip art peppered throughout, making everything look corny and outdated. Then you suffer an attack on your senses as a neon explosion hits your eyes. At least the color schemes have jarred you awake. Oh wait, there goes some flying text. There's a word slowly being spelled out as it does some acrobatics across the slide. I'm dizzy. Hang on, what's this presentation about again?

"Your slides should be a billboard, not a document."

– Lee Jackson, motivational speaker and presentation coach

If you have ever experienced one or more of these egregious acts, you are sadly in the majority. I have also suffered the slow death of a thousand slides. To be honest, I have even committed a few of these infractions! As a recovering Death-by-PowerPointer, I have inflicted the same torture on my audiences.

As an administrator and educator in continuing education, I have delivered countless lessons and presentations to adult learners and many diverse audiences over the last thirteen years. I have also been on the receiving end of some mind-numbing presentations. Time slowed to a crawl, and no end was in sight.

I am the first to admit that I was not a very engaging presenter in the beginning. I committed my share of Death-by-PowerPoint crimes. I packed in way too much information with bullet points everywhere. I dropped in several images for visual effect and even included some fancy transitions. That was what I was accustomed to seeing and what my peers were practicing. That was the norm. It didn't occur to me that all my genius and the extra information I was giving for free was not helping the audience at all. It strikes me as a little ironic that, as educators dedicated to lifelong learning, we are completely missing the mark in delivering our messages. We are all subject-matter experts in our own fields and have innovative ideas to share. Yet we are failing miserably on the execution of our ideas. We are essentially pouring our fountain of knowledge into a tumbler, and the cup runneth over!

"When you throw up bullet points and then run through them, you're guaranteeing that whatever you say will be quickly forgotten.

Not because you're bloody boring, but because people can't read and listen at the same time."

– Geoffrey James,
contributing editor, Inc.com

Back in 2017, I was so bored listening to a conference keynote speaker that I wanted to plot my escape from the room. But alas, I was the president of the association, and there was no way to make a stealth exit without being noticed. The speaker launched into another slide, jam-packed with figures and data. I could see the audience furtively looking at their watches. If I could have inserted thought bubbles above the crowd, most of them would probably have echoed my sentiment, *When is this going to end?*

While the keynote speaker was extremely knowledgeable in his field of labor market statistics correlating to training needs, the information was overwhelming to digest. It was too much, too abstract, and was forgotten the moment he stopped talking. I realized then what was lacking in the presentation. *Connection.* He spoke at great length about what he knew, but what I heard made me wonder how it related to me. It didn't move me or pique my curiosity, so I tuned out. And therein lies one of the missing ingredients of presenting. You must make people care about your message for them to engage.

I also noticed some common threads among the presenters. Many did not have a process for putting together their presentations. They thought (mistakenly) that they would just put up their findings on a slide with bullet points and use these as talking prompts to wing it. Unfortunately, what ended up happening was that they read from the slides and said the most obvious and superfluous thing, "As you can see from the slide...." The majority were also first-time or novice presenters and simply followed the common practice to which they had been exposed as being the norm. Thus the vicious cycle perpetuates.

It was time to take action. As someone who presents regularly, I could no longer do unto others what was done to me. These people gave me their time and attention, and I wanted to honor that by making sure it was worth their while and left a memorable impression. So I began changing the way I presented. I developed a process to simplify the delivery of my message, and most importantly, connect with the audience. I tested it out in one of my training workshops. When I collected the evaluations at the end of the session, I was amazed by the comments and feedback I received. Many remarked how much they thoroughly enjoyed my session and the way the information was presented. It made them think about how they could apply on the job what they had just learned. By George, they actually got it! As an educator, hearing that makes all the lesson plans, glazed looks, and administrative paperwork worth the effort! One student even wrote, "Can we have Fern do all the other workshops?" Not to toot my own horn, but in seeing such responses, I could deduce that this group enjoyed my particular session because it was different from the others. They could actually use the information I gave them!

I continued to fine-tune the process and presented at conferences using the same method. The results were overwhelming. People approached me at the end of my session and continued to engage! Other presenters bemoaned being in the adjacent room as the guffaws of laughter from the audience distracted from their presentations. Then they started asking me how they could get the same level of engagement with their audiences. And that is how this book was born.

Recall all the times you have endured painful presentations that would cure even the most stalwart insomniac. You don't want to be *that* presenter. It takes incredible courage to stand up in front of an audience and speak to your knowledge. But without the proper method, much of your brilliance will not be transmitted to the audience, and all your effort will be for naught.

I am challenging you to break that cycle. Now is your moment to stand out from the sea of Death-by-PowerPointers and make an indelible mark with your expertise. I will help you illustrate your points powerfully, building a connection to your audience. That is, after all, what PowerPoint was designed to do. But somehow, its application has been relegated to a de facto teleprompter.

In this book, I guide you through a step-by-step process that will propel you from your current state to being a memorable badass presenter. Within these pages, you will find Power Pointers (i.e., tips and helpful guidance) and Power Prompts (action items you can implement to engage your audience in-person and in a virtual setting). By the end of the book, you will have an action plan that will transform you into a confident, engaging presenter who can make the message stick!

YOUR NEXT STEP:

 ☐ **Accept the mission**

So buckle up, and let's begin your transformation!

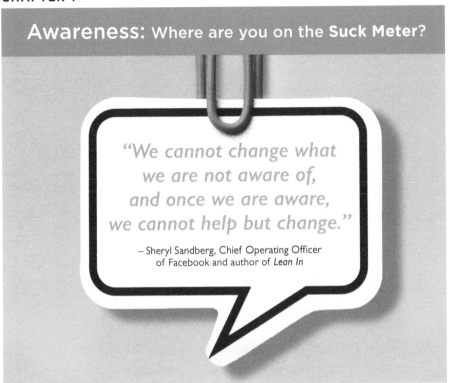

CHAPTER 1

Awareness: Where are you on the Suck Meter?

> "We cannot change what
> we are not aware of,
> and once we are aware,
> we cannot help but change."
>
> – Sheryl Sandberg, Chief Operating Officer
> of Facebook and author of *Lean In*

No matter who you are, whether you are a novice or seasoned speaker, you can always improve your current state. You wouldn't be reading this book if you didn't think you needed help! As the grand poobah of business management, Peter Drucker, said, "If you can't measure it, you can't manage it." In other words, you can't possibly get better at something if you don't know where you are beginning. Just like losing weight, you first need to step on the scale to measure your current weight before you can see how much you lost.

So let's establish your baseline and how far along the **Suck Meter** you are. Don't be discouraged at this point. Wherever you are, you can always make progress!

WHERE ARE YOU RIGHT NOW?

Let's take a trip down memory lane and think back to your last presentation. How do you think you fared on this scale?

1. **I did awesomely!** The audience was engaged from the beginning; they all laughed at my corny jokes, participated in the activities, and got my message! I received thunderous applause at the end, and I felt like a rock star on stage!

2. **It went well, I think…** No one got up and left the room. I got through all my slides and everything I wanted to say, and a few hands went up for questions. I saw smiles and nods. I feel good; I think I'll keep at it!

3. **Ooh…. That was a bit touch and go.** Good thing I was standing behind the lectern, or I wouldn't have been able to read my notes to know what to say! I lost a few people who got up to use the bathroom and never came back, but no one fell asleep, at least.

4. **It was horrible!** I was so nervous at the beginning that I forgot to introduce myself. I thought I was going to be sick, and time seemed to drag on. It was all a blur, and I couldn't wait for it to be over. I ran out of time and rushed through the end. I couldn't remember half the things I had to say, and I don't think the audience remembered anything either!

Your score: _____

AWESOME PRETTY GOOD TOUCH AND GO I SUCK

S U C K   M E T E R

MY PERCEPTION VERSUS REALITY

I have quite a healthy dose of self-esteem and always believed I was a decent presenter. Certainly not the worst, and enthusiastic enough to get a crowd engaged. After watching a video of myself presenting, though, I was shocked! I saw all my idiosyncratic behaviors come to the surface when I lost my rhythm or was stumped by a question. I noticed how often I looked at the slides instead of the audience. I also periodically crossed my arms without being aware I was doing it. I looked so defensive! The worst was when I heard myself unconsciously saying the words um and ah repeatedly! It was as annoying as hearing a valley girl say, "Like, you know…."

I cringed every time I heard myself utter those seemingly innocuous syllables. After watching the video, I felt terrible that the audience had to sit through all my filler words. I focused so much on the content and getting my point across that I didn't pay any attention to my body language and overall stage presence. So I took stock of my presentation from two perspectives, style and substance.

STYLE

I have seen presenters who barely look at the audience. They read through their slides with no variation in tone or volume—hanging on to the lectern for dear life, afraid of the audience as if they were about to pounce on them like prey.

POWER POINTER

No one will feel inspired if you enter the room with shoulders slumped, looking at your feet, and avoiding eye contact with the crowd.

I have seen amazing presenters who owned the room the moment they walked in because of their poise, confidence, genuine smile, and warm hello. I automatically smiled back and instantly responded, "Hello." It was the most natural thing to do, and the presenter had already engaged the audience before she even started talking. She had me at hello, and I was eager to hear more.

POWER POINTER

Seeing the audience smile back at you will help settle some nerves. From the beginning, set the tone that you are in charge and know your stuff.

CHECKPOINT #1:
What is your stage presence?

All eyes are on you as you stand in the spotlight to give your presentation. How are you presenting yourself?

You only get one shot to make a first impression. Following are some simple things to keep in mind to set the tone from the beginning. You have control over many aspects to ensure that the odds are in your favor. Start with your closet. Yes, you want to dress for success, but you must also feel comfortable. Wear something that makes you feel and look good. A clean, pressed shirt that is sharp and crisp looks great under any lighting. Don't appear with a wrinkled shirt or a ketchup stain on your tie. The audience will be so fixated on your poor appearance that they won't be focused on what you have to say.

For the ladies, wear something fitted that gives you a nice silhouette. You can wear a simple black sheath dress with a pop of color (e.g., red belt, colored scarf) to draw attention. You want people to see you when you move around the stage. If you will be standing for a considerable amount of time, make sure you wear sensible shoes for the occasion. When I know I have to stand for thirty to forty minutes, I opt for my low-heel shoes that give me just a little boost. I love my three-inch power pumps that are stylish and look great on the cover of Vogue, but they will make me absolutely miserable and preoccupied with discomfort. Sure, they make my calves look great, but no one is looking at them while I'm facing the audience! There is nothing worse than having pinched toes, trying to look elegant and composed, when all I want to do is kick them off my feet and slip into warm fuzzy slippers.

If you are going to grace the stage after being introduced by another person, you really want to put your best foot forward here, literally. Even if you feel nervous on the inside, you can project that confidence by dressing sharp, standing tall, and walking with confidence as you take center stage. Look at the audience, give them an acknowledging wave and a big smile.

CHECKPOINT #2:
How do you sound?

**You have garnered the audience's attention.
It's time for you to speak. How do you sound?**

It's not just about what you say. How you say it can play a big part in getting the listeners to trust you and buy into your message. How are you relaying your message to the audience? Are you animated and passionate about the topic, so your enthusiasm radiates to the crowd? Some rather technical presentations about law and statistics I've attended can cure insomnia in a heartbeat. But occasionally, I am pleasantly surprised. I once saw a statistician who was so excited about the facts and figures that I instantly perked up. He was talking about the story behind the numbers. The figures came to life. He built up the momentum and sped up to add urgency to the current crisis. Then suddenly, he paused and went quiet. I leaned in like a five-year-old, wanting to know what would happen next as I waited for him to resume. I was never interested in geo-spatial crime mapping before, but now I wanted to know how to find the hot spots based on the numbers!

That is how powerful your vocal attributes can be. Think of your voice as an instrument. You don't want to use just one note throughout the entire performance, the same repetitive beat with no change in dynamics. You need to add some crescendos, pauses—some syncopation to jazz things up a bit. Having dynamics in your voice and knowing when to speak softly or vary the pace can have a big effect on your audience. Nobody wants to listen to a drone.

Another thing to be mindful of is your frequency of using fillers when you are speaking. They are such a natural part of our speech that sometimes we aren't aware of how they sneakily creep into our presentations. Before you realize it, you are filling in the space between sentences with words like um, er, ah, like, well, I mean, you know. Even worse, you may string them all together when you are lost for words! Using these fillers can grate on the ears of your listeners and make you sound unsure of yourself. There is a simple fix if you are an um-er or an ah-er.

Record yourself the next time you are rehearsing your presentation and note each time you use a filler. What is the most common one you use? When do they appear most in your speech pattern? Once you know this, you can be aware that you are about to use a filler word and stop yourself. Leave a pause and see how that sounds when you play back your presentation. It's absolutely fine to have a moment of silence in your delivery. It's like having some white space on a billboard; you don't have to crowd every bit of it with words or images, and having some breathing room for your eyes helps you see the message more clearly. It's the same with the spoken word. Leave some strategic pauses for the message to sink in.

> *"Well-timed silence hath*
> *more eloquence than speech.."*
>
> — Martin Farquhar Tupper,
> English writer, poet, and author of *Proverbial Philosophy*

CHECKPOINT #3:
How is your body language?

Your body language speaks volumes before you even open your mouth to utter a word. How do you move? What are your facial expressions? What gestures do you use? Your body language contributes to your overall stage presence and will help you engage with your audience. Depending on the set-up of your venue, you should have an open space allowing freedom of movement, so the audience can see you completely. While it may be comforting to use a lectern for your note cards and then cling onto the side with an iron grip to steady your wobbly knees, it closes off access to your audience. You are also more likely to look down at your notes and avoid eye contact. People like to be seen, so acknowledge your audience by looking at them regularly. It also builds trust, and you cannot build that connection if you are glued to the lectern. You want to maintain an open posture free of any barriers between you and the audience. If you have to use a laptop or other media device to upload your presentation, you don't want to be held hostage standing by the computer to advance your slides. Use a remote, so you still have the freedom to move.

Whenever I am presenting, I keep moving. I like to move around the room and sometimes sit with the audience if I'm playing a brief video clip. This way, I can experience it from their point of view and be one of them. I am a very animated speaker. I love talking with my hands, and I have the worst poker face. Rather than tame these traits that are part of my personality, I work them to my advantage. I use gestures to reinforce important points and let my facial expressions tell the story. (It also helps that I am a shameless ham and have taken to the stage many times.) For example, if I list several items, I use my fingers to count them off. If I'm talking about something small, I hunch my shoulders over, making small, tiny gestures with my index finger and thumb. Find areas in your presentation where gestures will come across as natural, and use them to highlight key points or emphasize a concept.

Your entire body is a communication beacon, so be mindful of the signals you're sending. If you are nervous, you may unconsciously cross your arms and give off a defensive vibe without even realizing it. Or you may put your hands in your pockets or behind your back. This gives the perception that you are hiding something you don't want the audience to see. Take a video of yourself the next time you are rehearsing your presentation. Watch for these cues or other unconscious actions you may exhibit out of habit. Note your posture.

How are you standing? Do you slouch or hunch your shoulders? How often are you making eye contact with the audience? Do you use your hands to talk? How can you use gestures to fit what you are saying?

POWER POINTER

Watch Neil deGrasse Tyson's MasterClass in *Scientific Thinking and Communication*[1]. He effectively uses gestures and his whole body to communicate technical matters about space. He is so engaging that you are instantly drawn into the experience as you watch his hands tell the story of stars and planets.

SUBSTANCE

Now that you have taken stock of the style, let's see how you measure up regarding the content of your presentation.

CHECKPOINT #4:
Quality of Content

Most presenters use a presentation program to deliver their talk, the most ubiquitous being PowerPoint and other contemporaries such as Prezi or Keynote. When you are to present, it is almost expected that the organizers will ask for a slide deck. Overhead projectors and transparencies are relics compared to these modern-day conveniences. All you have to do is click a button, and a slide full of information can pop up on-screen. The question is, how are you using the program to relay your message?

---

[1] https://www.dailymotion.com/video/x7wl1pe

No doubt you have experienced presenters who put everything up on the screen—full paragraphs, copious lines of text, charts, graphs, and everything in-between crammed into their slide decks. Then the presenter treats the full-screen slides like a teleprompter and reads them word by word. It's the greatest irony that what was intended as a "smart" and convenient technology has inadvertently made people less smart and more dependent on using it to do everything for them. Remember, *you*, not the program, are the one delivering the message.

> ### *"PowerPoint makes us stupid."*
> – General Stanley A. McChrystal,
> former head of US and NATO force

The material you put on the screen should be nothing more than a prompt for your talking points. It acts as a visual guide for the audience to understand your message; it is not a teleprompter for you or the audience to read along.

If your presentation looks like what I described above, you are not alone. I have been there too and ranked pretty high on the **Suck Meter** in my early days. However, it wasn't until I reviewed my performance on replay that I realized I was a Death-by-PowerPointer! Experiencing my presentation like an audience member made me want to squirm and bolt for the door. That realization prompted me to change the way I presented.

POWER PROMPT

Your turn to take stock

If you have a recording of a presentation you have given, this is an excellent opportunity for you to take stock of all the checkpoints above. If you do not have one, use an existing presentation you have delivered, and record yourself. Dress for the part, and run through the presentation from beginning to end. When watching the replay, note your delivery (style) and the quality of the content (substance).

STYLE	OBSERVATIONS
How do I look?	➤ I look confident and comfortable in my own skin… ➤ I'm like a fish out of water…HELP!!
How do I sound?	➤ I use a lot of ums and ahs… ➤ I sound natural
How is my body language?	➤ I have a tendency to …
SUBSTANCE	
How does my slide deck look?	➤ A lot of bullet points… ➤ I am giving a lot of information… ➤ I am using/not using visuals properly

POWER PROMPT Checklist

✓ Think of the audience experience and ask yourself the following questions:

☐ How would I feel listening to my presentation as an audience member?

☐ Would I be engaged by what I'm seeing and hearing?

☐ Do I want to plot my escape? (Hopefully not!)

Download the Observation checklist from
www.fernchan.com/powerprompts

WHAT'S THE POINT?

Looking at oneself in the mirror can be a bit of a shock to the system, but it is the first step toward progress and improvement. Be kind to yourself when you are taking stock. Set your mind to making progress, not perfection.

Now that you know where you are, let's move on to building the foundation of a kick-ass presentation.

CHAPTER 2

The Preparation Formula: How to use C3PO

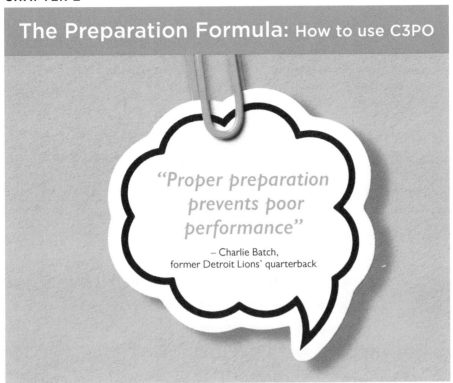

"Proper preparation prevents poor performance"

– Charlie Batch,
former Detroit Lions' quarterback

For those of you who are Star Wars aficionados, you are probably wondering what the lovable and somewhat pedantic human-cyborg-relations droid, C3PO, has to do with presentations? Apart from the fact that he is fluent in over six million forms of communication, his name provides a handy formula for setting up a framework for success.

C3PO FORMULA

To spell it out simply, you need Clarity (C) on the Purpose, People, and Place (3Ps) to deliver Only what they need to know (O).

Let's break down the formula and see how the mechanics work.

C = Clarity

Be crystal clear about what you are presenting. This means making your content easy to understand so the audience follows what you are saying. When you speak with clarity, the people in the room will understand and receive your message. If they don't get it, they are going to lose interest fast. In short, people will keep listening if they see value in the information, but only if they understand it and relate to it. So let's apply the C to the 3Ps, the purpose, people, and place.

> *"If you can't explain it simply, you don't understand it well enough."*
>
> — Albert Einstein,
> theoretical physicist and mathematician

P1 = Purpose

What is the purpose of your presentation? What is the problem you will solve or bring to light? What is the message you want your audience to understand at the end? You should know how to answer these questions succinctly and with conviction.

As humans, we are self-serving creatures. We do things to better ourselves and improve our lot in life. Think of the acronym WIIFM (i.e., what's in it for me?). This self-interest is a high motivator and you can channel the purpose to meet that interest. What is it you want your audience to know that they don't yet know? What actionable steps do you want them to take at the end? How will this information benefit them?

For example, you are making a sales pitch for your product. What do you want your potential buyers to know? At a minimum, you want to explain what your product is, what the benefits are, and how it can help them. At the end of your presentation, you want to illustrate how your product can help improve their lives or solve their problem. The benefit to them is of such high value that without it, their pain won't go away. Your product can give them relief, now.

Always come back to this question when you are preparing your presentation, "How will the desired outcome or conclusion help the audience?"

Making sure you meet this purpose highly depends on the next P, the people.

P2 = People

Who is the audience? Are these your peers? What is the common interest that brings them together? The more you understand your audience, the better they will understand you.

Designing a presentation without an audience in mind is like writing a love letter and addressing it to whom it may concern."

– Ken Haemer,
former AT&T presentation research manager

Think of it this way, why are they here to listen to you? Hopefully, they didn't just randomly waltz into your room by mistake, looking for the speaker in the next room instead! Are you reporting your annual strategic goals to staff, and they have no choice but to be there? In that case, you really want to get your message across because your bottom line will most likely be at stake.

There is an intended audience for what you have to say, whether they are volun-told to be there, or they want to attend. In any event, you have to understand that it is all about them. They are the focal point, and your message must speak to their pain or passion. Get to know your audience and learn about their backgrounds and motivations. You can work that information to your advantage by tailoring your talk to build rapport.

As you are speaking the same language, you can relate to them on a meaningful level. This, in turn, will help with engagement. How you interact with your audience and build rapport also depends on the next P.

P3 = Place

Location, location, location. Where and when are you presenting?

Knowing your location in advance and what the room set-up looks like will help you plan your movements. Get to the venue early to see the space so you can familiarize yourself with the surroundings. Give yourself ample time to set up. Plan for any contingencies or adjustments you may need to make for your presentation, and if possible, gather advance information about the venue such as:

➤ **Room size**
(e.g., conference room, classroom, auditorium)

➤ **Seating arrangement**
(e.g., round-table, rows of chairs, theater seating)

➤ **Technical set-up**
(Is a media cart provided, or do you have to bring your own laptop and related equipment?)

➤ **Light sources**
(Does the room have windows where natural light may be too bright for your visual aids? Are there curtains or blinds you can adjust? Can you dim the lights if you need to show a video?)

➤ **Possible distractions**
(Can people walk in and out of your room easily? Does sound carry over from another room?)

Not all venues are primed for hi-tech, modern-day conveniences such as Wi-Fi. In one of my seminar tours, I had a last-minute change of venue to a basement room. It was the only space big enough to hold the number of attendees. I hadn't expected this change, and a part of my presentation involved playing a video. When you are in the bowels of the earth under slabs of concrete, you are lucky to have one bar of connectivity on your cell phone, let alone the ability to stream a video from YouTube! In another instance, I was in a hotel venue that had all the conveniences. But alas, all the guests were also taking full advantage of the amenities, such as the free Wi-Fi, and I was mired in the slow spinning wheel of connectivity. I have since learned to embed any media so that whatever audio or video clip I show will not depend on the internet connection.

If you are presenting in a virtual setting, you will have to make different preparations. This topic will be covered in depth later, in Chapter 6.

P3.5 = Placement

Along with knowing the lay of the land, it is equally important to know when you are speaking and how much time you have been allotted. Unless you are the keynote speaker and given a prime time slot, you will rarely have the option to pick your preferred time. In addition, the time of day will heavily influence the state of your audience. So make the necessary tweaks and maximize your engagement accordingly.

Being the first speaker of the morning is ideal. People are generally most alert and are bright-eyed and bushy-tailed. But as you get later into the morning and closer to lunchtime, your audience will start feeling hungry. They will lose concentration faster as the rumbling in their stomachs takes over their senses. If you are in the mid-morning session, work in some audience engagement midway through so that they have something else to think about.

If you are getting an after-lunch crowd, be aware that they will be digesting their lunch, may not be most attentive, and could drift off into ZZ-land! Design your presentation with some dynamic interaction at the beginning so they are involved and can be snapped out of their lethargic state. You may also want to consider bypassing slides and dim lights. Instead, use some old-school methods like a flip chart. Call upon a volunteer to be a scribe, or engage the audience in some other form of active participation.

The mid-afternoon, or last session, can be the most challenging time. People lose concentration again, thinking about the end of the day and other preoccupations. I know I struggle to stay awake at 3:00 p.m. and can appreciate the custom of having an afternoon siesta! An effective way to manage waning interests and wandering minds is to address it head-on. Use some humor to acknowledge that your audience may be fatigued and falling asleep. People are usually surprised at such candor, but they can appreciate that you are saying what they are feeling. Then dial up the passion and energy in your delivery. If you built in some question and answer time toward the end, don't feel you have to use up all that time. Remember when you were let out of school early and how excited that made you feel? People don't mind if you finish early.

Finally, there are the evening and weekend slots. Surprisingly, people are more likely to be attentive because it is outside of office hours. That means they have chosen to be there on their own time, rather than out of work obligation. Thus, you need to be most respectful of this time frame. They are probably bypassing personal and family obligations to listen to you, so make sure that what you are presenting is worth the sacrifice of their free time.

O = Only What They Need to Know

Don't overwhelm your audience with too much information. They may come to you as empty vessels, but they can only retain so much before all those facts and figures spill over into the abyss of forgotten information. Not to mention, most people have terrible memories!

Instead, *focus only on what they need to know*, rather than the nice-to-know extras. The brain seems to work best thinking in threes, so apply the rule of three to have the most impact on your listeners' memories. What are the three main points of your presentation? What are the 3Ps in the formula? (See what I did there?)

If you are bold enough, you can even try to boil it down to one single idea, so you can explain it in great depth with all your passion behind it. Make the audience care about it as much as you do. Explain your idea by expanding on it piece by piece, so it all connects. This is one of the reasons why TED Talks are so successful. They zoom in on a single idea, and everything links back to it in some way—and they do it in under twenty minutes. (I highly recommend the book TED Talks by Chris Anderson to supplement the increase of your presentation skills.)

POWER PROMPT   Fill in the blank

For your upcoming presentation, apply the C3PO formula:

C - Clarity:
I will make my content easy to understand so the audience can follow what I'm saying. I will do this by applying the 3Ps.

P1 - Purpose:
The purpose of my presentation is to

_____

P2 - People:
The audience I am presenting to are

_____

P3 - Place(ment):
I am presenting at (location) _____

(in person or virtually) _____ and I am

speaking for (minutes) _____ at (time) _____.

O - Only:
I will give the audience *only what they need to know by applying the rule of three.*

Download the free C3PO Formula from
www.fernchan.com/powerprompts

WHAT'S THE POINT?

By applying the C3PO formula, you can design your presentation with greater clarity and precision regarding what you have to say and to whom you are saying it. Knowing the time and place will give you the additional context to shape your presentation to maximize your audience engagement. You will also set clear boundaries for the amount of information you are giving. Remember that what you are talking about has to speak to your audience (it's all about them) and not your wealth of knowledge on the topic (it's not about you).

These are the building blocks of your presentation that will set you up for the next phase of organizing your materials.

CHAPTER 3

Structure Your Material: Get your house in order

"Good order is the foundation of all things."

– Edmund Burke, author of
Reflections on the Revolution in France

Once you have established your building blocks, the next step is to gather your information and provide a clear structure for your delivery. Just as baking a cake requires logical steps to get the raw ingredients to the finished product with icing on top, your presentation must be structured clearly to lead the audience from point A to point B. You need to know what you are going to say and the order in which you will say it.

Be a good storyteller

When you organize your material, build your structure as if you were telling a story. Whatever you are presenting, remember you already have an intended audience for this information. Your goal is to impart your knowledge and get the people to follow along.

When you weave your information into a story arc, it is the perfect vehicle to take your listeners from the starting point to the final destination. Having a narrative structure will help you engage your audience because we are hard-wired to listen to stories. Telling a personal anecdote and how it relates to the central message is a far more effective way than presenting bullet points on their own without context around them.

> *"Story-telling is the most powerful way to put ideas into the world."*
>
> – Robert McKee,
> author, lecturer, and story consultant

Every story has a beginning, middle, and end (rule of three in action). Your presentation needs to behave the same way, so let's structure it accordingly.

BEGINNING—Introduction

Like any good story, you begin with the plot. Who is the main character? What is the obstacle they have to overcome? How are they going to do it?

How to apply it to a presentation:

1. Introduce the topic to your audience
2. Tell them the problem
3. Explain how, by the end, you will get to the solution

Use the introduction to set expectations with your audience. Explain to them how you have organized the information and what they will take away. Tell them if they can ask questions throughout the presentation or should wait until question and answer time. This will give the audience a preview of what will be covered, what to expect, and what you want them to get out of it in the end.

Example:

When I presented to educators at a virtual conference on presenting virtually, I could not have asked for a more synchronous audience. Right off the bat, I told them I was going to:

1. Share my ninja moves to improve their presentation skills in a virtual environment

2. Explain the problem that online audiences have shorter focus and are falling asleep behind the screen

3. Provide simple hacks they can use to get the audience to engage immediately and to make the lesson stick

MIDDLE—Main Message

Now is the exciting part of the story where all the drama, action, and intrigue take place. This is where you expand on your main idea. Focus on the most important thing first. Provide the supporting material to make your case (e.g., data, case studies, analysis). Arrange your key points in logical order. You want to build up some anticipation of what will happen next and then lead to a natural conclusion.

Example:

> Continuing with the presentation cited above, I expanded on the three components. First, I used examples of worst-case scenarios and common pitfalls to illustrate the problem. Then I provided simple fixes using simple technology and media that they could implement in their presentation, and I showed them how to make it all work on a webinar platform.

END—Conclusion

The end of the story is where it all comes together, and loose ends are tied up. Summarize your message and conclude with the key points that you want your audience to take away. Did you help solve the problem? Did you bring awareness to the problem? Tie it back to the purpose of your presentation, so it comes full circle. People like a definitive end to a story. Don't leave them hanging with any unresolved questions!

Example:

> At the end of the presentation, I repeated the focal points from each component. Then, I summed up the key takeaways and tied it all back to how they could use it to level up their presenting skills.

Write it out

Once you have outlined your introduction, main message, and conclusion, draft a script for your story. Some people are natural orators. They know their topic so well they can speak off the cuff and improvise without a script. If you are one of these gifted individuals, I applaud and admire you. But for the rest of us mere mortals who don't want to leave it to chance and draw a complete blank, or waffle on aimlessly, I strongly recommend a script. What do you want to say, and how will you say it? What stories, anecdotes, or metaphors can you use? Think about the language that best meets your audience where they are. Is there a shared vocabulary that you all understand? Be mindful of any technical jargon or acronyms you are using. For example, you may know that APEC stands for the Asia-Pacific Economic Conference, but it could easily mean the Annual Pie-Eating Contest to someone else. If using acronyms, be sure to explain what they stand for so everyone is on the same page.

Check for flow when you are done. Does the script easily lead the audience from one point to the next? Remember, you are talking through the ideas, and your audience is listening. Even though you are scripting your talk, it should sound natural and conversational when you say it out loud. It shouldn't sound like you are reading it. You are speaking to what you know from the heart, so you can deliver it with passion.

Storyboard it

Look back through your script. What images can you use to represent the concept or idea you are conveying? Imagine your presentation like a movie production. What are the stills you can use to set the scene and tell the story? A good example is to use pop-culture references such as movies, memorable characters, or well-known songs to make your story come to life. When people recognize what they have seen or heard, they can form an association with your content. However, be very thoughtful about what you choose as a reference point. Just because I am an avid Star Wars fan doesn't mean everyone will understand the image of Luke Skywalker doing the Jedi mind trick to represent the concept of influence. Hard as it is to fathom, there are people out there who have not seen a single Star Wars movie.

Figure 1: Luke Skywalker using the Jedi mind trick on Bib Fortuna to let him into Jabba the Hutt's lair.

By selecting the appropriate images and other visual aids to match the narration, you will significantly improve what the audience recalls about the presentation. This is because the information is being absorbed and processed by more than one level of consciousness in the brain—what researchers call "dual-coding." Many PowerPoint presentations hit the **Suck Meter's** all-time high because there is very little to help visualize what they are hearing or make it memorable. So let's avoid that common mistake and add some scenery to our journey.

"Organizing is what you do before you do something, so that when you do it, it's not all mixed up."

– A. A. Milne,
author of *Winnie-the-Pooh*

POWER PROMPT Checklist

✓ Organize - Get your stuff together

☐	**Structure**	Structure your presentation into three sections
☐	**Introduction**	What is the story?
☐	**Main Message**	What happens in the story?
☐	**Conclusion**	What happened in the story and how it ends
☐	**Draft**	Draft a script for narration that is natural to say—do not read
☐	**Storyboard Your Presentation**	What images can you use to convey the idea?

Download the Organize checklist from
www.fernchan.com/powerprompts

WHAT'S THE POINT?

Having a clear structure will help the audience to get from point A to point B and not get lost in between! Now that you have your script, and have curated some images to match, let's dive into the next chapter on making the most of the visual aids to tell your story.

CHAPTER 4

How Visuals Help: It's as simple as show and tell

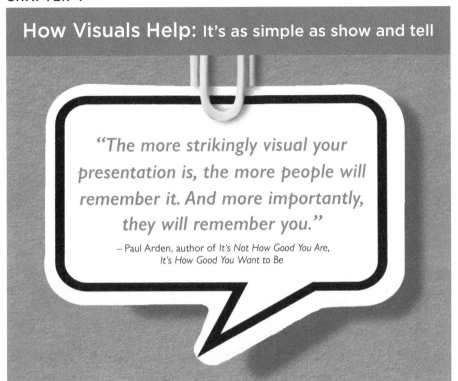

"The more strikingly visual your presentation is, the more people will remember it. And more importantly, they will remember you."

– Paul Arden, author of *It's Not How Good You Are, It's How Good You Want to Be*

I'm sure you have heard the saying, "a picture is worth a thousand words." When you look at a picture, there are colors, details, depth, and so much information that can be absorbed in an instant. But if you had to describe the image, it might take up to a thousand words. No one wants to read that on a slide! That is why visual aids can be so compelling when you are presenting. They can capture the imagination and evoke emotion in the audience.

Although visual aids can be impactful, I want to share a word of caution. Too many images can be overwhelming but poor representation can be underwhelming. Using visuals needs to be done with purpose, not as an afterthought. There is a bit of an art to using visual aids, but most people do not use them effectively. In fact, I have seen many presentations where images are just dropped into the slide alongside the bullet points, together with cheesy clip art. My senses have been assaulted by some garish color schemes, where my instant gut reaction was to grab the barf bucket. I have seen a dizzying array of flying slides, disappearing slides, bouncing letters, spinning words, and all manner of transitions because some presenters are determined to use every single transition that PowerPoint offers. This is a sure-fire way to score high on the **Suck Meter.**

In this chapter, I will walk you through how you can effectively use visual aids and audio-visual media. You don't have to be a graphic designer to create amazing images. You can do this yourself with the right tools and know-how.

Think in pictures

I think of the best examples of visual aids when I am doing storytime with my children. I am often amazed at how they can sit still, so engrossed in the story. I have read Eric Carle's *The Very Hungry Caterpillar* to them more times than I can count and can even recite it in my sleep. They can't read at ages two and four, but they can follow along. How is that? Because they are looking at the pictures and connecting the images with the words as I am reading aloud. Pictures tell a story, and as adults, we still function the same way. That is how you need to think about using visuals in your presentation.

I give a lot of thought to image selection and how I can use them to tell a story. One of my favorite examples is an image of a toilet paper roll with its last sheet hanging on. Right above the image are the words, "Oh sheet!" When I show this full-bleed image on the screen, I love watching the audience's response just to see what registers. The first reactions I see are usually some chuckles and acknowledgement. Who can't relate to this situation? I know I have been caught in this predicament, while panic sets in that I am in some deep doo-doo! I then ask the audience about their initial feelings when they saw the picture. Did you feel a sense of dread? Did you think, *Uh-oh, I'm in trouble?* Did you ask yourself, *What else can I use that is nearby?* More chuckles ensue. From just that image, I was able to get an emotional reaction from the audience. I am connecting with them at a very organic level through a natural function we all experience. Then I frame the message I want to convey. And that is how I introduce the managing of situations in crisis.

How does this image represent the story I want to tell?

Figure 2: *A little toilet humor to arouse a sense of dread and emergency to introduce the topic of crisis management.*

Engage the five senses

You can say a lot with an image. Leave it up to the imagination of the audience to make the association as you provide the narrative. This will save you from having to put multiple bullet points on a slide. Remember, this is not a read-along. Choose a meaningful image that will evoke emotion in your audience. Think about your five senses as you are doing so. Picture this. I put up a full-bleed image of a burger and a side of fries. There are plump buns and a thick, juicy patty with melted cheese draped beautifully over it. In addition, two slices of crispy bacon rest on top of the cheese. Next to the burger are some golden, thick-cut fries.

Did the image make you feel hungry? Did you want to take a bite out of that juicy burger? Could you smell the fries? The point here is to connect with your audience so that your message is memorable. As one of the leading coaches for brain health, Jim Kwik, says, "picture plus emotion equals long-term memory." Nobody remembers boring things; they remember things that make them feel powerful emotions.

"I've learned that people will forget what you said, people will forget what you did, but people will never forget how you made them feel."

– Maya Angelou,
American poet, memoirist, and civil rights activist

I know this might seem a little counter-intuitive, but sometimes words can pack a punch as well. What gets lost in this execution is the use of too many words. The audience is experiencing eye fatigue. No one wants to read ten lines of twelve-point font stretching from one end of the slide to the other and carrying on to the next line. Instead, think of putting one word or a quote that people know to conjure the image. Always ask yourself, "Will the words arouse some emotion? Will it raise some eyebrows and pique curiosity?"

Now amplify that word or quote and make the font a minimum of thirty-point. Use an easy-to-read serif font like Arial. You want to read that word or phrase clearly from the back of the room. Seeing the word "Hungry?" will instantly make you think about your stomach and images of what you want to eat for your next meal. You may have thought about a juicy burger with fries or something else quite delectable. On seeing the word "Hungry?" I have activated your sense of taste, smell, and even sight as you picture what you want to devour come chow-time.

➤ Use an evocative image to tell the story. Think of the emotion you want to arouse when you are using this picture. How do you want the audience to feel when they see the picture? People remember how they feel, not necessarily what you say

➤ Use a high-resolution image. Think about how it will look when projected on a large screen or in a big auditorium. You don't want it to be grainy, or worse, have a copyright watermark in the background. You can get free high quality resolution images from websites such as pixabay.com and unsplash.com

➤ Use your image as a full bleed so it occupies the whole screen and can make that maximum impact when your audience sees it. You can overlay any text you want to include, but make it brief—not a long list of bullet points

➤ One image or idea per slide. Use icons where possible to represent the idea or word

➤ Avoid any clip art in your visual aid. These look extremely outdated and add a level of cheesiness that will inch you forward a few points on the **Suck Meter!**

➤ Be mindful of clashing color palettes or colors that are not color-blind sensitive. If in doubt about what colors to use, pick a pre-assigned palette from PowerPoint. These have been designed with complementary colors that work well together. You can use them safely without fear of causing nausea

➤ Limit your transitions to one or none per slide. Too many bouncing letters and waiting for spinning images to appear will throw off your timing and induce more dizziness and nausea for the audience

A moving image

Beyond still images, you can also use a combination of audio-visual media to engage your audience. To introduce a topic or to show relevant examples that connect to your message, it is so easy to find instructional videos, snippets from your favorite movie, or real-life scenarios on YouTube to embed in your presentation. You might have your own video footage that illustrates the point. By seeing you in action, the audience may appreciate that you are practicing what you preach, whether you were successful in your attempt or not. They also give you a break from speaking and the opportunity to observe the audience reaction as they watch the screen.

When I use a video clip, I always set it up for the audience, so they know the context and what to expect. I like to give them a heads-up and explicit instructions if I want them to look out for something or simply to observe the clip as a further explanation to my narrative. Just as with images, I am equally intentional with what I choose to show and how it relates to the audience. In one of my workshops that I present to security guards to test how observant they are, I love showing them a short video called the *Monkey Business Illusion*[2], which you can find on YouTube . The instructions from the video are simple.

"Count how many times the players wearing white pass the ball."

The scene opens with six people, three of them are in black t-shirts, with one team member holding a ball, and three are in white t-shirts, also with one member holding the ball. They pass the balls to their team members as they move around each other. After several passes, the round is done, and they all exit the stage. The solution is then given to

[2]https://youtu.be/IGQmdoK_ZfY

the audience, "The correct answer is sixteen passes."

Then it continues,

"Did you spot the gorilla?"

Gorilla? What gorilla? Is this a trick question? Believe it or not, about half the people don't see the gorilla because they are so focused on counting the passes that they miss it entirely. This experiment was originally designed by Christopher Chabris and Daniel Simons, who explain how our brains trick us into thinking we see and know far more than we actually do. The security guards who spotted the gorilla felt immense validation about their observation skills and how vigilant they were, but the half that didn't—let's just say they were glad their supervisor wasn't in the room!

Like a captivating image, videos can be highly effective when the audience members relate to them and engage with the content, whether it pertains to their professional lives or a shared everyday experience. In the above example, I am asking a group of security guard officers, who are trained to observe their surroundings, to put their skills to the test in a simple task of counting how many passes the players in the white shirts make. By tapping into their knowledge and skill set, I am setting up the scenario to get their buy-in, so they watch the video with vested interest and follow the instructions as prompted. I always get a strong reaction from the crowd afterward; they are surprised by the results, one half of the room thinking, *How did I miss the gorilla?* and the other half thinking, *How could anyone not see the gorilla? It was right there on center stage!* That buzz from the audience creates great energy that will spur your presentation on, providing you with a captive audience that is intrigued and wanting to know more.

Can you hear me now?

When I use audio clips, I like to prime my audience first and ask them to put on their listening ears. As I give them simple instructions on what I want them to listen for, this adds a little intrigue. In this instance, you are tapping into their sense of sound. Observe your audience and see how many of them close their eyes or lean in to hear a little better. Engagement is a two-way street. You should always observe how your audience is reacting so you can adjust your delivery to make their experience enjoyable and memorable.

I find using audio clips particularly useful in virtual presentations, especially if you need a little icebreaker to test whether your audience is familiar with the platform and how they can interact in the remote setting. You can play a brief clip of a song and ask your audience to name it in the chat box. You could do a few of these snippets to get your listeners' attention and get them to take part. I also like including people who speak English with different accents, saying things that are colloquial to their land that would be a bit of a head-scratcher for others who aren't familiar with such sayings. What was said, what you think you heard, and what you interpreted as the meaning can lead to some interesting discoveries, and now you have an audience wanting to hear more.

Going old-school

Beyond these technical methods, some old-school visual aids are equally effective. Flip charts! If you are to employ this method, you need to make sure the audience can see what you are writing or drawing—and that your handwriting is legible. If you are in a big lecture hall and look like an ant on stage, then the flip chart may not be the best medium unless there is a camera on you, and it can be magnified to the crowd. But in a small, intimate setting, flip charts are a great way for you to show on the spot what you know. Illustrate the image and make the connection from point A to point B for your audience. One of the best examples of how to use a flip chart effectively is Simon Sinek's *How Great Leaders Inspire Action*. This TED Talk[3] has had over fifty-five million views. He talks for eighteen minutes and illustrates his Golden Circle idea succinctly on the flip chart.

POWER POINTERS

➤ **Use dark colored markers to write so that it will pop on the white paper**

➤ **Write big and legibly**

➤ **Make illustrations simple (you don't have to be Leonardo DaVinci—stick figures are okay!)**

➤ **Position your body and flip chart so you are not turning your back directly to the audience**

➤ **Stand to the side of the chart to write or draw what is necessary**

If you are in a setting that has a whiteboard, you can use this as you would a flip chart. The advantage of using these old-school methods is that you are moving from one spot to another. So if you are standing

[3]https://www.ted.com/talks/simon_sinek_how_great_leaders_inspire_action

behind a lectern or a podium, you must move to the flip chart stand or the whiteboard. We are programmed to follow motion, so when you move from one spot to another, the eyes of the audience follow you. Have you ever seen a tennis match? While the audience watches the ball bounce from one side of the court to the other, their heads turn from side to side as they track it.

I'm not saying that you have to run from one end of the room to the other to get your audience to follow you, but make use of the surrounding space. For example, as you walk evenly across the room, pause for a minute to look straight into the audience. Their eyes are already fixed on you, and now you have a moment to look at one person and make a connection.

Another tried and true old-school method is an actual demonstration. Using a simple prop, you can give some physical context to an otherwise intangible concept. One of the most effective demonstrations I give utilizes what is already in front of me. At most conference events where I present, there is a pitcher of water and a glass set on the table for the speaker. When I speak on the topic of how to be a better presenter, I use the glass and pitcher to portray the effects of too much information. The glass represents our capacity to hold information. The pitcher holds all the information and knowledge about the topic at hand and is visibly higher in volume. But once the glass is full to the brim, all that extra information, regardless of how important or fascinating, will have no place left to go but to spill over as wasted wisdom. Remember the O in C3PO? *Only give them what they need!*

POWER PROMPT   Checklist

✓ What you can use to show and tell

☐ Hi-resolution images (absolutely no clip art)
☐ Images or words that arouse the five senses
☐ Video and/or audio clips
☐ Flipchart or whiteboard to write or draw (old-school methods still work)
☐ A prop for demonstration

Download the Show and Tell checklist from
www.fernchan.com/powerprompts

WHAT'S THE POINT?

To sum up, the human brain processes information more effectively when images accompany narration, rather than only text and narration. If I put a word like "abstract" on a slide, it is a very intangible concept and hard to describe. But if I show an image of Jackson Pollock's style of splotchy painting, most people would connect the meaning of abstract art to the word and think of it as something you can't quite describe as an object or as concrete, and is kind of "out there." When you can combine the words with visuals, whether it is a still image, video, live illustration, or demonstration, you anchor that idea in the mind with meaning and connection. Using our innate love of story-telling coupled with visual harmony is the secret sauce to making your message memorable.

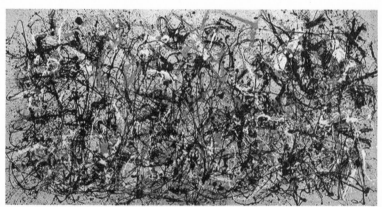

Figure 3: Conceptualizing the meaning of abstract with Jackson Pollock's artwork Autumn Rhythm, 1950.
https://learnodo-newtonic.com/jackson-pollock-famous-paintings

CHAPTER 5

Data Presentation: What to do with facts and figures

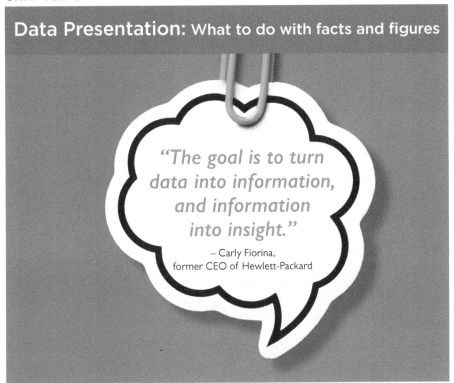

"The goal is to turn data into information, and information into insight."

— Carly Fiorina,
former CEO of Hewlett-Packard

Presenting data is usually the kiss of death and the most effective way to lose your audience. Data is informative and important, and we are constantly making data-driven decisions. Or, at least, we like to say that we can't make decisions until we see more data. We want statistics, figures, comparisons, and numbers to convince us that what is being offered is worth its weight in gold. Because we are so convinced of this, we happily oblige our adoring audiences and present them with graphs, charts, and numbers in detail! On the whole, whenever I see data presented, I want to put out a bat signal to be rescued. The majority of data being presented today is the biggest contributor to Death-by-PowerPoint.

In this chapter, I am going to help you reverse this trend and make data appealing (yes, it is possible). I will also show how you can present it in a way that will save your audience from the inevitability of the Grim Reaper's scythe.

"The problem isn't finding data,
it's figuring out what to do with it"

— Mike Loukides,
Vice President of Content Strategy for O'Reilly Media, Inc

The goal when presenting data is to make it engaging, easily digestible, and relatable. Yet many presenters do the complete opposite with boring representations and overwhelming information. While it is tempting to supply the excess data because it is there, too much can overload and confuse your audience. Remember, our minds work better with breathing room and space to absorb information.

An effective way to cure this common malady is to strip the data down to its core message and simplify it. Remove any extraneous "chart junk" like legends, extra grid lines, multiple lines, and other embellishments to your figures.

Looking at the example cited by *Presented*, a UK company specializing in PowerPoint presentation designs, you can see how the same data can be presented in a simpler way that is easy to grasp.

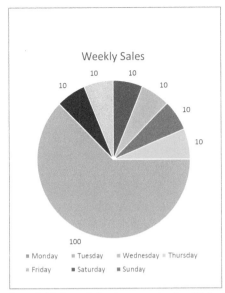
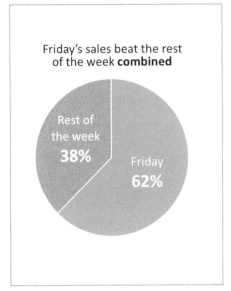

Figure 3: A before and after chart comparison from UK Company Presented.
https://presented.co.uk/wp-content/uploads/2019/01/Chart-comparison-4.png

The pie chart on the left is a fairly standard example. It has a heading and colorful segments of the pie that make up the whole. But now I have to figure out the legend and what days belong to what color. I am straining to see the extremely small font. This is already taxing my brain, and there are no concrete figures to tell me what I'm supposed to learn from this pie chart. It is pretty to look at, but it lacks clarity regarding the data.

When I look at the chart on the right, however, in an instant, I can understand what I'm looking at. The heading is clear. It tells me that sales on Friday did better than the rest of the week combined. The word combined is in bold, so it draws my attention to an important fact about the data point. The pie chart is clearly segmented into two sections. The bigger chunk is in blue, and the smaller chunk is in gray. There are two labels (Friday, Rest of the week) with corresponding figures (62%, 38%). The data points are highlighted by using a larger font in bold. This is data done right.

Here is a brilliant example from astrophysicist Neil deGrasse Tyson on how 130 billion dollars would look like in earthly terms.

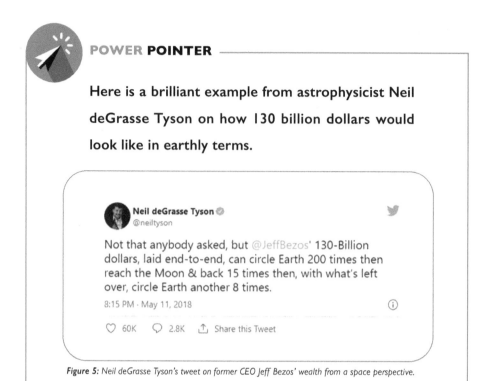

Neil deGrasse Tyson ✔
@neiltyson

Not that anybody asked, but @JeffBezos' 130-Billion dollars, laid end-to-end, can circle Earth 200 times then reach the Moon & back 15 times then, with what's left over, circle Earth another 8 times.

8:15 PM · May 11, 2018 ⓘ

♡ 60K   ♡ 2.8K   ⬆ Share this Tweet

Figure 5: Neil deGrasse Tyson's tweet on former CEO Jeff Bezos' wealth from a space perspective.

When you can compare a data point to something tangible and relatable, it will help your audience connect with the figures rather than get lost in them.

Working in higher education, I can tell you that we are inundated with boring data, surrounded by faculty members who love to show their research. They are often the biggest offenders in showing endless screens of data. Data is crammed into bullet points or complex charts with big numbers. Some report their findings in the most unappealing presentation with so many data points that I have turned off and tuned out. And these are my peers! I can only imagine how tortured the students feel who have to sit through a session.

Not to insult my higher education colleagues, I, too, have committed the same faux pas, thinking that sharing such compelling data would move the audience into shock and awe. I was providing extra information! And who doesn't like more stuff for free? It's like a bonus! In reality, I was just spouting off numbers, providing no tangible context that would make a connection for the audience.

In one course I teach around mental health, I use a lot of data to show the severity of depression in the United States. I thought I was ahead of the game by localizing the data to New York, as it is my home base. And so I put up a slide with a bullet point that says, "Depression is found in approximately 7% of New Yorkers."

Figure 6: *An early example from my Death by PowerPoint days when I used cheesy clip art, bullet points and too much text*

To give that statistic more context, I included a clipart image of a baseball stadium with the following caption:
"18 Yankee Stadiums could not hold all the of the New Yorkers with a lifetime diagnosis of depression."

Yes, I am embarrassed to admit that I used outdated clip art. In addition to that, there is a glaring typo in the caption that makes me cringe at the sight of it. Just because I am writing this book about how not to suck at presenting doesn't mean I didn't suck at one point, making the same mistakes I now teach against. I wondered why the audience wasn't moved when they saw such high numbers. I thought maybe they weren't Yankees fans and rooted for the other home team, the Mets. Or maybe they weren't into baseball. Still, if you live in New York, especially in New York City, you know Yankee Stadium.

Then I realized I wasn't making an emotional connection for the audience. What was a generic clip art image going to do to make the audience realize the immensity of the problem? Nothing. Nada. Zip. Zilch. Zero. So I reworked the slide, removed the bullet point and tacky clip art, and instead used an actual image of Yankee Stadium at its full capacity of fifty-thousand people. The audience can see that the stadium is packed to the brim with real people seated in the stands. I gave them a visual context, and most of them can imagine themselves in the picture, seated in the nosebleed section, paying for overpriced beer and hotdogs. Then I overlay the following text in the picture, "Yankee Stadium x 18". Now I prompt the audience to multiply that image eighteen times in their mind. As they picture it, I narrate the mathematical equation.

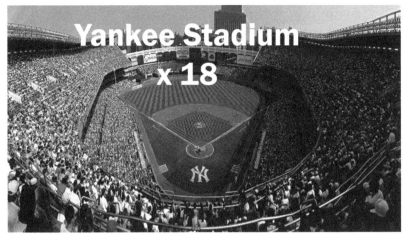

Figure 7: Depression reimagined in a full-bleed image of Yankee Stadium multiplied by 18. Depressed yet?

"A sold-out crowd at Yankee Stadium of 50,000 x 18 = 900,000 people. Can you imagine that eighteen Yankee Stadiums at full capacity are still not enough to hold all the New Yorkers with a lifetime of depression?"

I get a much different response when I present this particular statistic because they can grasp the magnitude of the problem and meaningfully understand that number.

If you are presenting any data, keep these three things in mind:

1. What is the purpose of the data?

Think about what the data is showing.

Is the number going up or down?

Is there a trend or pattern showing?

How does this data point tie into your main message?

2. How do I make it relatable?

Numbers can be staggering. Help connect the audience to that number by comparing it to something they understand and feel.

3. Keep it simple.

Less is more. Strip the data down to its core message. Remove the "chart junk."

Download the Self-reflection questions from
www.fernchan.com/powerprompts

RESOURCES:

There are many other books and resources available that address how to present data in a clear and simple way. I recommend Garr Reynolds' book *Presentation Zen* and Nancy Duarte's *Slide-ology* for further examples. For helpful blogs on data visualization, check these out:

This blog explains what data visualization is and beautifully illustrates how it can be represented in different ways for reports, presentations, marketing, and more:
https://venngage.com/blog/data-visualization/

For practical tips on how to present complex data in PowerPoint:
https://presented.co.uk/data-visualisation-tips-powerpoint/

This guide is helpful for examples of how to present numbers:
https://www.mauriziolacava.com/en/presenting-data/presenting-data-in-powerpoint/

In addition to Nancy Duarte's Slide-ology, check out her blog post on How to Display Data Correctly in Presentations:
https://www.duarte.com/presentation-skills-resources/display-data-in-presentations/

WHAT'S THE POINT?

Just as I did in the previous chapter in using a compelling image to tell a story, I am using the same technique here with data. I used a very iconic image that my New York audience can recognize and gave them a visual representation so they can understand the scope and meaning of the numbers involved. People won't engage with the content if they can't understand or relate to it.

This is where a lot of presenters lose their audience when presenting data. They assume the attendees will understand what they are looking at and do mental arithmetic on the spot to get to the same conclusion. When I see complex numbers and charts, my brain switches off because I don't want to do any number crunching. I want the presenter to do the math and lead me to the natural conclusion. I did not expect my audience to calculate what 50,000 times 18 equals. Instead, I described it and gave them the final number, so they didn't need to do the math. Now they have the answer and understand how that figure represents the number of New Yorkers suffering from depression.

CHAPTER 6

Presenting Virtually: Different medium, different tools

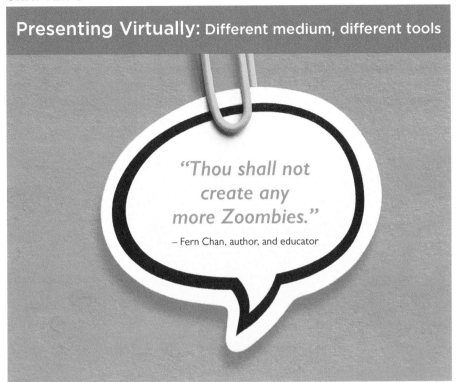

"Thou shall not create any more Zoombies."

– Fern Chan, author, and educator

Long before we zoomed in and out of classes, meetings, and calls, I sat through countless Zoom meetings, attended many virtual conferences, and conducted numerous webinars over the years as an educator. Thanks in part to the COVID-19 pandemic, people are now more accustomed to working and learning remotely. Though we were quick to adapt to this new mode of connecting with our friends, family, peers, clients, students, and employees, keeping an audience engaged has proven more challenging.

Besides all the regular pitfalls of presenting, we are now faced with managing all kinds of technical issues inherent in virtual presentations.

Before you throw your hands in the air and give up, rest assured that you don't need to be a tech whiz to present remotely. But you do need to understand some of the challenges and what you can do in a virtual environment to level up your presentation and engage your audience. Are you ready, Player One?

THE VIRTUAL CHALLENGE

What to do with technical difficulties

Some of the most common and vexing problems of presenting virtually are the technical issues beyond your control. Poor internet connection at your location can suddenly cut you off while you are presenting. It can also happen to your audience, who drop off like flies and never return to your session.

By far the most sweat-inducing, anxiety-ridden experience I had was when I lost my Wi-Fi signal in the middle of my presentation to a full class of thirty students. I was getting into my flow, progressing through my talk, when suddenly the screen froze. I was clicking my mouse furiously, tapping all sorts of keys as if I was performing CPR on the keyboard to get some life back into the screen. I knew there was nothing I could do at that point until the server rebooted, and it felt like an eternity waiting two minutes to reset everything. Then I logged back into the Zoom platform and hoped I still had an audience waiting to resume the session and that the system had not kicked everyone out of the class. Thankfully, the majority were still there. I lost a couple, but those who stayed on were a very sympathetic group of adult learners accustomed to these technical difficulties, and they gave me a few more minutes to regroup and pick up where I had left off.

But there was another glitch. I was not the host of the meeting and couldn't share my screen. The organizer, who was the original host of the meeting, had granted me co-host privileges at the beginning and was no longer there. Since I was disconnected, I did not automatically maintain co-host status when I re-entered the virtual meeting space. I felt my scalp getting itchy, my armpits getting sweaty, and panic about to set in as my internal voice was cursing up a storm. Then I took a deep breath, smiled, and explained to the group that the technical gods were not with us at this moment, and we would carry on in a more conversational style.

The big lesson from this experience? Remember that your slide deck is nothing more than a visual aid. I know my topic inside and out, and now I get to engage the audience differently by asking more probing and reflective questions and getting direct feedback that way. It wasn't how I had planned it, but seeing all the faces and names on my screen also allowed me to address a person by name if they had questions.

Nobody knows your presentation and its message better than you. So if all else fails, talk to your audience. If they turned the camera option on, address them face to face, so to speak. If that is not an option, use the chat function. Say the question or comment aloud and respond accordingly. This way, you are also acknowledging the audience member and can thank them for participating.

One technical challenge you have control over is knowing the platform you are using. Whether it is a video teleconferencing platform like Zoom, WebEx, or Microsoft Teams, or a webinar platform like GotoWebinar, WebinarJam, or Demio, having some familiarity with the system will help you immensely with your delivery. You will want to know what tools are available within the platform and how you can effectively use them for engagement in a virtual format. Take the time to learn the functionalities of the platform that will help with interactions. Many of these have common features such as a chat box, polls, breakout rooms, and spotlights to bring an audience member on as a guest speaker. Your seamless transition will not only help the audience participate virtually, but you will also maintain your flow without needless interruptions like figuring out what to click and where to find it. Work the system, so you won't get lost searching for the toolbar to access the features you need.

When in-person tools of engagement don't work

Traditional methods of in-person engagement are tricky to translate directly over to a virtual setting. Back in the pre-pandemic days, when I presented in person, I had the freedom to move about the classroom to draw attention through the motion. I would walk around and stop casually in front of an unsuspecting student who was falling asleep, and he would bolt straight up again. It was also easier to get the entire room to participate in icebreaker activities, as I could physically orchestrate the audience to do what I wanted.

But in a virtual space, I don't have the luxury of moving around, or sensing the energy in the room, or seeing who is falling asleep. People also have a hard time concentrating when looking at a screen for long periods of time. As it is, the human attention span is shorter than that of a goldfish these days, lasting less than twelve seconds before getting distracted. So watching a talking head for one hour is a lot to ask of someone, especially in this environment. The majority are also taking part from the comfort of their home, where other distractions are abundant. From boisterous children to barking dogs, the drama from home is competing with your screen time.

If you have a one-hour slot to present, I recommend speaking for only forty minutes. You need to allow for some late arrivals at the start, potential connectivity issues, and other technical delays that will eat up a handful of minutes from your time. With a shorter time frame to work to, you also need to include plenty of interactivity to keep your audience glued to the screen. Here are four simple ways you can instantly engage your audience in a virtual setting.

1. Use the polling feature

Most people will be familiar with using Zoom as a mode of delivery for webinars. Within Zoom, as with other webinar platforms such as Demio, and WebinarJam, is a polling feature that will enable you to post some questions for a quick audience response. In my experience, launching a poll at the beginning of the presentation is an effective way to warm up the audience and get them to collaborate early. It sets up an expectation that the presentation will be interactive.

I like to infuse some humor into my question and the multiple choice answers (if appropriate) just to see if they choose the most outrageous option. It's also a convenient way to test the system and the audience's familiarity with the platform, so they know what to do and how to respond. When they actively have to click something, you have gained a focused audience.

POWER POINTER

Have your questions planned out and uploaded into the platform ahead of time, so you are not creating them on the fly. You want to hook your audience from the get-go and not fumble about typing the question and answers while presenting. This will help you with your timing and with how polished you are in the delivery.

2. Use the Annotate function

Figure 8: To annotate, look for the pencil icon in Zoom when you are screen-sharing.

When you are screen-sharing in Zoom, there is an *Annotate* function that you can use to draw your audience's eyes to a particular area in your presentation. It works like a stylus, where you can choose your nib width and color to write, draw arrows, circle words—and more—to make a point of emphasis in your presentation. You can also use the whiteboard function to illustrate your points. I find doing simple math on the whiteboard to be quite effective, especially when the audience can see my thought process when carrying the one over in my arithmetic. I've also hand-drawn three concentric circles and indicated where they all intersect in the middle as a significant point of synergy. This is a brilliant way to create that motion for your audience to follow in lieu of you moving across the stage or around the room.

 POWER POINTER

Practice using the Annotate tool prior to the presentation. Because you will use your mouse as a stylus, your handwriting will not be as impeccable as you might like. Even drawing simple shapes like circles, arrows, and checkmarks can prove to be more challenging than you would imagine. Test out the various stylus widths and colors that will work best against your slide and contrast nicely when you annotate.

3. Embed an audio clip

 I love to embed audio clips into my presentations as part of an interactive activity. I will ask the audience to put on their listening ears, give them explicit instructions on what I want them to listen for, and that they should note what they heard. Not only does this drum up some intrigue, but I have also given them clear directions to follow so they can verify if they have the right answer at the end. Most of the audience will perk up a little and lean in to listen with concentration so they can take notes. Sometimes I use simpler icebreakers, such as playing a short clip of my favorite 1990s tunes and asking the audience to name the song or singer in the chat box. (I like to use Virtual Insanity by Jamiroquai as an example, go figure!) Using audio clips will get your audience to listen and guarantee participation.

POWER POINTER

Test out your audio clip in the platform prior to your live presentation so you can click *Play* on the screen and have the audio clip run. Some webinar platforms will only import images and text from PowerPoint, but not multimedia. This will require a separate upload, so prepare for that if the platform doesn't support embedded presentations.

4. Embed a video clip

 The same concept applies here as it does in person, as explained in Chapter 4. Show a "how-to" video or a brief clip from the news or a movie that relates to your presentation and draws in your audience. Just as with the audio clip, ask your audience to watch for certain things or ask some reflective questions at the end. Again, give clear instructions on what you want them to do during the video. You can easily run the Monkey Business Illusion example here, and for added engagement, include a poll on how many saw the gorilla.

POWER POINTER

As with the audio clip, make sure that if the video is embedded, it will play seamlessly on the platform. If it has to be uploaded separately, you will want to save your videos so you can access them easily. When screen sharing in Zoom, enhance your media by checking "Share computer sound" and "Optimize screen sharing for video clip."

You can go a long way in engaging your audience using these four simple methods without getting too overwhelmed with the technology. As with anything new, preparation and practice are key to ensuring all these things run smoothly for the presentation, especially if it is your first time doing it virtually. The next chapter will go into further details about the run-through, but for the purposes of this chapter, do a practice run of your presentation on the platform with a test audience. Get the timing down, and build in any necessary debriefing after each engagement piece. If you find an activity too clunky or confusing for the audience to follow, you can make the adjustments now or cut the activity. Make sure to mark your time when you are done and see if you are over or under your time limit. Remember to have some buffer and not talk for the entire hour!

Helpful tools of the trade

Once you have worked out all the content, there is an external component that you also need to consider for optimizing your delivery. This requires a small investment in equipment, but it will make a world of difference in how you look and sound if you're going to be doing more virtual presentations in the future. Here are three essential tools to consider.

1. External microphone

Investing in an external microphone will instantly improve the sound quality of your presentation. This is especially important if it will be recorded. Most internal microphones on a desktop or laptop pick up a lot of external noise, like typing on the keyboard or your neighbor mowing the lawn. They are positioned too far away from where you're seated, and the sound quality tends to be tinny. You certainly don't want to be leaning toward your screen to speak into an invisible microphone while the camera captures you at unflattering angles.

2. Webcam

Using a webcam mounted on the top of your screen will give you better control of angles and viewing ratio of your face. With an internal camera, the position is fixed, and again you will be held hostage to odd angles, where the top of your head may be cut off, or you are too far from the screen. Some laptops have the camera built in at the bottom of the screen, so you have to prop the laptop up at eye level or tilt the screen to see your entire face. These scenarios create more unflattering angles from double chins to gratuitous boobs shots.

3. Lighting

Never underestimate what good lighting can do to make you look good! Have a source of light behind the camera or computer, whether it is a window or translucent light bulb. You want your face to be well lit from the front, so you don't have any five o'clock shadows. Don't prematurely age yourself if you don't have to. If you are going to be recorded, you don't want to look old and haggard and have that video out for posterity.

POWER PROMPT Checklist

✓ Get your tech-savvy on

- [ ] **Familiarize yourself** with the virtual platform. Know what features are available and how you can use them

- [ ] **Use polls** to engage the audience. Prepare those polls in advance

- [ ] Use the **annotate function** to draw or write. Practice using the tools

- [ ] **Embed audio or video clips** with clear instructions on what you want the audience to listen to or look for

- [ ] **Practice** using these features before going live. Know what to click and where to find the buttons

- [ ] Get your timing down. **Know how long your presentation is** from beginning to end

- [ ] Set up an **external microphone**

- [ ] Use a **webcam** for better angles

- [ ] Have a **good source of light** behind the camera

- [ ] **Know your material** so well that if all technical features fail, you can still engage with your audience through conversation!

Download the Tech-savvy checklist from
www.fernchan.com/powerprompts

WHAT'S THE POINT?

Virtual presentations are here to stay. Even when in-person activities resume, conducting meetings, conferences, and classes through a virtual platform is part of our lives. Presenting in person and virtually will not be mutually exclusive. Having the ability to do both will make you a more flexible and appealing presenter. Now let's bring this all together with the last step, the dress rehearsal.

CHAPTER 7

Putting it all Together: The dress rehearsal

"Practice isn't the thing you do once you're good. It's the thing you do that makes you good."

– Malcolm Gladwell, Canadian journalist and bestselling author of *The Tipping Point*

Practice, practice, practice!

Congratulations! You have reached the most exciting part of the process, the delivery! Once you have organized your presentation, written your script, gathered the images and any other visual aids, it's time to breathe life into your presentation and rehearse it. The key to a smooth execution is practice. Lots of it. If you were going to a Broadway show or a concert to see your favorite artist, you would expect a polished performance, right? None of these artists would ever step on stage unprepared and wing it. Your presentation is no different. It is a performance, and you want it to be a pièce de résistance!

Many people make the crucial mistake of not rehearsing—taking for granted they know their material and what they are going to say. There is a big difference between running it through in your mind and saying the words out loud.

Now it's time to get on stage and perform your masterpiece. Let's get the show on the road and run through the dress rehearsal checklist.

Be proud, say it out loud

This may seem obvious, but in case there was any doubt—say your presentation out loud. Saying the words out loud will help you get over any tricky pronunciations that you may not catch when rehearsing in your head. Seemingly innocent combinations can get your tongue tied up and sounding incoherent. As the subject-matter expert, the last thing you want to happen is to get choked up on words you can't pronounce. Ever tried saying, "red lorry, yellow lorry" several times? Now is also the time to catch any filler words that creep into your delivery. Those ums and ahs can furtively sneak into your speech patterns, but you never notice them when you are rehearsing in your head. Go back to your checklist from Chapter 1 and watch for where fillers may pop up, and make a conscious note to not say them. It is okay to pause and let peace fill their ears for a brief moment while the story sinks in.

Timing is everything

Get a feel for the entire presentation and rehearse it from beginning to end. Time yourself. You will often be surprised at how long it takes to get through everything. Are you within your allotted time? Most people overestimate how long they need to present and end up either rushing through their presentation, or worse, going over their time and keeping the audience hostage. Not only does this cause headaches for the event organizer, but it also takes time away from the presenters after you. Don't be a time-stealer. In my experience, if I'm still talking during my rehearsal at the fifty-minute mark for a one-hour time slot, I will shave another five to ten minutes off the presentation. It is essential to build in that extra time whether you are in-person or virtual, as you may have to account for some late arrivals, technical difficulties, debriefing of activities, and any questions and answers at the end.

The rehearsal will also give you the opportunity to test out any media you may be using. For example, if you have an audio or video clip to play, how long will it take to load? Familiarize yourself with the command buttons on the computer if you need to play any media, or use the remote pointer to help you with transitioning from one slide to the next. Especially in a remote setting, you will want to know what to click at the right time for the polls and other annotation functions and test how the engagement activities will work.

Get a live test audience

Get some willing participants to take part in your rehearsal as audience members. If you are stumped by who to ask, do not be shy about gathering your friends, family, or co-workers to be your test audience. People who are unfamiliar with your subject matter make a valuable test audience. They will point out gaps in your story, especially if you are making assumptions that they know certain things. If they can follow what you are saying, this is a great indication that you are getting your message across. Observe their reactions and level of engagement. Are they laughing at points where they should, or are you hearing crickets? Are they engaged and taking part in the activities? Are they listening with great interest or yawning and shifting in their seats?

You have a supportive crowd who wants you to succeed, so use that to your advantage. They will be far more forgiving when you slip up and will give you honest feedback so you can improve your delivery. Be open to hearing points of improvement from your test audience. Hearing about their experience and what they enjoyed the most or least will help you adjust where needed.

Fire up the passion

Nothing will motivate a crowd more than genuine passion and enthusiasm. The opposite is also true. If you are not animated and excited about what you have to say, it's going to be a hard sell to get your audience excited about it too. People feed off your energy. You will receive what you put out, so bring it! How did you appear to present? Did you bring passion and confidence to the floor? You may be presenting the most mundane topic, like the monthly sales report, but your enthusiasm and energy can instantly put the crowd in the same mood.

"Your enthusiasm becomes their enthusiasm;
your lukewarm presentation becomes
their lukewarm interest in what you're offering....
When the audience is bored, it's not their fault"

– Bill Walsh
American professional, and college football coach

Own your knowledge

Don't get on stage if you don't know your material and how you are going to deliver it! You should know your subject matter forward, backward, and sideways so you can answer questions about that topic with confidence and ease. But getting to that point requires consistent practice and not just a one-time run-through in your mind. Think of the most successful comedians who get up on stage to do stand-up. It is actually quite the opposite of being spontaneous and carefree. According to actress and stand-up comedian Margaret Cho, comedians are extremely calculated. They perform their jokes many times, often adding to them, tweaking them, taking words out, all to figure out how they can best present the punchlines. So while the audience experiences a roll-on-the-floor-almost-peed-in-my-pants belly laugh, it is the result of the presenter practicing the delivery of that joke over and over again.

Dress for success

It's a dress rehearsal! That means rehearsing the presentation in the outfit you plan to wear. You want to feel comfortable and confident in your clothes but also avoid any wardrobe malfunctions. (Refer back to your Awareness checklist in Chapter 1.) I recall one speaker who wore a new shirt, and when he stretched his arm to point to the screen, it ripped under the armpit! I have experienced a loose bra strap slipping off my shoulder and constantly having to adjust it during my presentation. While I'm grateful the presentation wasn't a complete bust (pun intended), I cringed when I saw how it looked on video. I seriously want a redo of that performance! If you know your presentation will be recorded for posterity and viewed online for a long time, then make sure you choose something that will make you look and feel good.

Be friends with your nerves

It is normal to feel nervous before a presentation. In fact, so many people are afraid of public speaking that they avoid it at all costs. So take heart that the audience will most likely understand how you feel if you make a little fumble. Acknowledge your nerves. As famous research professor, Dr. Brené Brown, teaches, there is power in vulnerability. It's okay to say, "Oops, I'm so nervous I forgot what I had to say!" They will want to root for you even more because they know it takes a lot of courage to speak in public.

Even though I am well-seasoned at delivering presentations, I still feel butterflies in my stomach every time I go on stage or enter a virtual room. But rather than let my nerves get the better of me and fight them, I accept them as a part of me. I think of it as my body signaling that these nerves just can't wait to get out into the world through my presentation. They are buzzing through my system, and I am going to channel the adrenaline into my message. I give myself a little pep talk, "I got this," and strike my Wonder Woman power pose. I'm now ready to kick ass.

If you are struggling to manage your nerves, there are a few things within your control that you can do immediately to take off the edge. As a certified Mental Health First Aid instructor, I know that one of the most effective ways to manage anxiety is to take a few deep breaths. Breathe in through your nose and fill your belly with oxygen. Then slowly exhale through your mouth for twice as long. The oxygen in your system will bring a sense of calm. Slowing things down will help you gain control of your racing heart and breath. Make sure you have a bottle or glass of water nearby as adrenaline causes your mouth to become dry. Drink some water to lubricate your mouth and pipes so that when you speak, your voice won't come out as a squeak. Be careful not to chug too much water, or you'll have to make a run for the bathroom! Now cheer yourself on. You've got this!

One last thing, have fun

Yes, seriously, have fun! Enjoy the ride through all the bumps, rough patches, and smooth sailing. Having fun is contagious, and when the audience sees you having a good time, they want in on the action too. If you are presenting like it's a laborious chore, no one will want to do it because it's not fun. Even if you have a few stumbles along the way, don't be discouraged. You can always learn from the "oops" and later transform them into "a-ha" moments. Remember that time flies when you are having fun.

"People rarely succeed unless they have fun in what they are doing."

– Dale Carnegie,
lecturer and author of *How to Win Friends and Influence People*

POWER PROMPT Checklist

✓ Your rehearsal checklist

☐ Say it out loud

☐ Set the timer

☐ Get an audience

☐ Fire up the passion

☐ Own my knowledge

☐ Dress for success

☐ Make friends with my nerves

☐ Have fun

☐ Repeat all the above several times

AWESOME PRETTY GOOD TOUCH AND GO I SUCK

SUCK METER

THE POINT OF IT ALL

So there you have it. You now have an action plan to make your presentation more engaging and stand out from the Death-by-PowerPoint presenters. I encourage you to keep practicing with these tools and fine-tuning the process. Consistent practice over time will help you master your own style of delivery and connect effortlessly with the audience. Learn from their reactions and feedback. At the end of the day, remember you are communicating information and that communication is a two-way street. Your sole purpose in presenting is to make sure the audience receives your message.

I want you to make a difference in the world around you with what you know. You have valuable knowledge and experiences to share with others and you now have the tools to make your lasting impression on the world. Go forth and own that stage when you present. You are a badass presenter!

The Force is with you.

APPENDIX

Here are some actual slides taken from my presentations *How to Transform Your Presentation from Meh to Wow* and *How to Virtually Up Your Presentation Skills* that illustrate many of the points in the book.

Slide 1: How to avoid this scenario - the all too familiar Death-by-PowerPoint

How Rivers Are Formed

- Rivers start as very small streams and gradually get bigger as more and more water is added. Heavy rains and spring meltwater add so much water to some rivers that they overflow their banks and flood the surrounding landscape.
- The water in rivers comes from many different sources. Rivers can begin in lakes or as springs that bubble up from underground. Other rivers start as rain or melting snow and ice high up in the mountains.
- Most rivers flow quickly in the steeply sloping sections near their source. Fast moving water washes away gravel, sand and mud leaving a rocky bottom.
- Rivers flowing over gently sloping ground begin to curve back and forth across the landscape. These are called meandering rivers.
- Some rivers have lots of small channels that continually split and join. These are called braided rivers. Braided rivers are usually wide but shallow. They form on fairly steep slopes and where the river bank is easily eroded.
- Many rivers have an estuary where they enter the ocean. An estuary is a section of river where fresh water and sea-water mix together. Tides cause water levels in estuaries to rise and fall.

Slide 2: Information overkill! Bullet points galore, small font, and text over image - a deadly trifecta with a high score on the suck meter.

Source: https://www.emaze.com/2020/08/22/6-worst-presentation-slides-ever

Slide 3: What to do instead. Use an image that speaks to the topic.
All the bullet points can be summarized on a hand-out, and given to the audience after the presentation.

bad color **schemes** can lead to...

- Distraction
- Confusion
- Headache
- Nausea
- Vomiting
- **Loss of bladder control**

Slide 4: Poor color choices that use all the colors of the rainbow.

Slide 5: Choose a color palette that is complementary and reflects your branding.

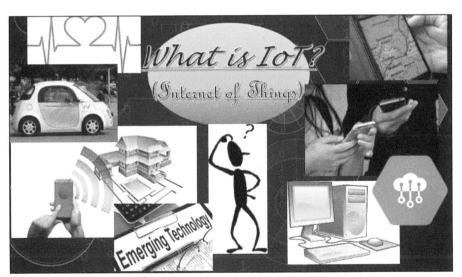

Slide 6: Too many images, cheesy clipart, hard-to-read font - another killer trifecta on the suck meter!
Source: https://24slides.com/presentbetter/bad-powerpoint-examples-you-should-avoid

Slide 7: Use a compelling image that evokes a strong sense of emotion.

Slide 8: Simplify to one idea/image per slide

Slide 9: Use a high-resolution image and extend to full bleed for greater impact

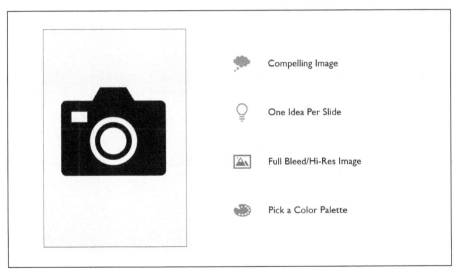

Slide 10: Recap slide on visuals. Use icons to summarize points.

Slide 11: When it comes to text and visuals, be zen. Less is more.

Slide 12: Use an audio clip to get your audience to listen. Give clear instructions on what you want them to do.

Slide 13: Insert a video clip. Again, give clear instructions on what you want them to observe.

Slide 14: Use the polling feature for virtual presentations to get audience participation.

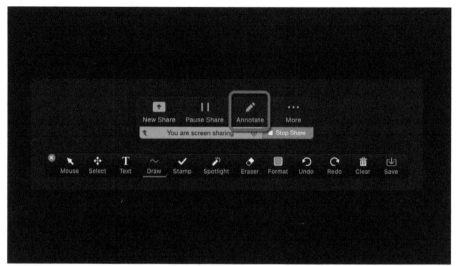

Slide 15: Use the annotate function to draw, highlight or write notes on the slide.

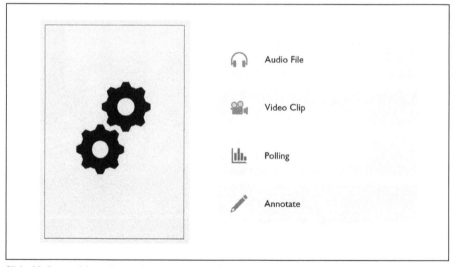

Slide 16: Recap slide on low tech engagement tools

Slide 17: Some hardware to boost your virtual presentations. Use an external microphone.

Slide 18: Use a webcam to capture better angles and ratio.

Slide 19: Never underestimate how lighting can make you look good!

External Mic

Webcam

Lighting

Slide 20: Recap slide of external hardware for virtual presentations.

ACKNOWLEDGEMENTS

*I am incredibly blessed to be
surrounded by so many people whose love,
support, guidance and patience have
made this book come to fruition.*

To my Dad, Charles, newspaper editor extraordinaire, who taught me the economy of words with his red-pen editing since my first book report at age 13. It was brutal at beginning Dad, but I know now it was because you held me to the same standards as your reporters.

Mom and Mei - The Chan women whose indomitable life force runs through my blood.

Artemis and Tiberius - my original masterpieces, who give me lifelong learning skills as a parent, and plenty of communication tactics and strategies!

My Wonder Women crew - thank you for always being there as my test audience, and providing valuable feedback for my presentations. You all rock!

Julia, my accountability buddy - I am in awe of your superpower planning skills! You inspire me to stay on track and to keep going.

Self-Publishing School - what an incredible infrastructure and support you have set up for aspiring writers to make their dreams come true!

Joy Roos Sephton - thank you for taking up the red pen, and putting the finishing touches on the proofreading.

Rachael Cronin - your talents never cease to amaze me as a designer.I love that "Rachaelize" button!

To my early audience - apologies for suffering through some of my earlier presentations where you may have been inadvertently bumped off.

Finally, to everyone on my launch team, thank you from the bottom of my heart. It means the world to me that you took the time to get a copy of my book, read it and write a review. I am so grateful for your support.

Thank You for Reading My Book!

I hope you enjoyed the book! I really appreciate all of your feedback, and I love hearing what you have to say.

I need your input to make the next version of this book and my future books better.

Please leave me an honest review on Amazon letting me know what you thought of the book.

If you have used some of the tips in the book for your presentation, please share your experience! Stay in touch at:

www.fernchan.com
Facebook @fernchanauthor

If you are looking for an engaging speaker to inspire others to be better presenters at a conference, meeting or virtual event, please reach out at **fern@fernchan.com**

Thank you so much!

Fern Chan

ABOUT THE AUTHOR

Fern Chan is an avid lifelong learner, working in the field of continuing education in New York City. A passionate educational advocate, Fern is focused on delivering impactful training with applicable skills to real-life situations that promote compassion, fairness, and mutual cooperation in today's world.

Never one to shy away from center stage, Fern is also a shameless ham who loves to perform, present at conferences and participate in mud races.

She lives with her husband William, and two rambunctious children Artemis and Tiberius.

Milton Keynes UK
Ingram Content Group UK Ltd.
UKHW051324181223
434593UK00022B/254